ZODIAC SIGNS

# ARIES

## March 21 – April 19

Jennifer Howse

AV2
www.av2books.com

Step 1
Go to **www.av2books.com**

Step 2
Enter this unique code
**PMGSRMN8U**

Step 3
Explore your interactive eBook!

AV2 is optimized for use on any device

# Your interactive eBook comes with...

**Contents**
Browse a live contents page to easily navigate through resources

**Audio**
Listen to sections of the book read aloud

**Videos**
Watch informative video clips

**Weblinks**
Gain additional information for research

**Try This!**
Complete activities and hands-on experiments

**Key Words**
Study vocabulary, and complete a matching word activity

**Quizzes**
Test your knowledge

**Slideshows**
View images and captions

## ... and much, much more!

ZODIAC SIGNS

# ARIES

## March 21 – April 19

## Contents

# Are You an Aries?

Do people call you independent? Are you always up for a challenge? If this sounds familiar, you might be an Aries. An Aries is someone who was born between March 21 and April 19.

Aries is a sign in the zodiac. This is a series of 12 **constellations** that run across the night sky. For centuries, people have used these groups of stars to tell the future. The study of the stars in this manner is called astrology.

# Zodiac Chart

**A person's zodiac sign is determined by his or her date of birth. Which sign matches your birthday?**

# It's in the Stars

The zodiac constellations form a circle around Earth. In one year, Earth makes a full **orbit** around the Sun. As it does this, the Sun appears to be in different places at set times. The zodiac constellations are found along the path the Sun appears to follow.

Long ago, people used the Sun to tell the time of year. In late March, the Sun passed through the Aries constellation. People born then were said to be born under the sign of Aries.

Over time, the position of the constellations shifted. Even though the Sun now passes through Aries at a different time, the dates associated with the sign of Aries remain the same.

Aries is the **39th largest constellation** in the night sky. Its main shape is **made up of four stars**. At least **54** other stars are found within it.

The brightest star in the constellation Aries is **Alpha Arietis**. Also called Hamal, it is **two times more massive** than the Sun.

The Aries constellation is also known as The Ram. It is one of 42 constellations that represent an animal.

# The Myth of Aries

The ancient Greeks had stories about how each zodiac constellation came to be in the sky. Aries is linked to the **myth** of the golden **fleece**.

When Ino married the king of Boeotia, she decided to get rid of his two children, Phrixus and Helle. She arranged for Boeotia's wheat crops to fail. This caused a famine to fall over the land.

The king sent a man to the city of Delphi to seek advice from a priestess there. Ino found the man and bribed him to lie to the king. He was to say that the priestess promised the land would recover if the king sacrificed his children to the gods.

Zeus, the king of the gods, heard about the bribe and sent Aries, the winged ram, to save the children. Aries swept down, wrapped the children in his golden fleece, and flew them to the land of Colchis. Upon their arrival, Phrixus gave the ram and its fleece to Zeus. As a reward for Aries' brave act, Zeus placed the ram in the sky as a constellation.

People came from far away to seek the advice of Delphi's priestess, the Pythia. She could be found at a temple there.

# Aries and Cardinal Signs

In astrology, some zodiac signs share certain **qualities**. These qualities show how a person acts in the world. The qualities are separated into three groups. Cardinal signs are great at kick-starting projects. Fixed signs can be counted on to finish any project they start. Mutable signs bring their creative spirit to their work.

Aries is a cardinal sign. People in this group are ambitious. They like to set goals for themselves and those around them. Fixed signs are also competitive. They like to come in first, whether they are climbing a mountain or taking a test.

The competitive nature of an Aries can be seen at both work and play, even during a friendly game of tennis.

# Zodiac Signs
## by Quality

### Cardinal Signs
Love to think big.

Aries

Cancer

Libra

Capricorn

### Fixed Signs
Keep things organized.

Taurus

Leo

Scorpio

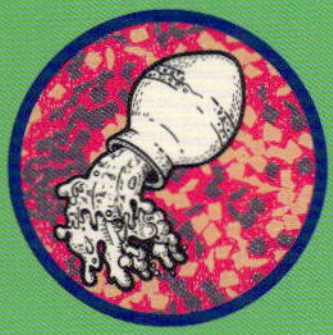
Aquarius

### Mutable Signs
Are thoughtful and full of dreams.

Gemini

Virgo

Sagittarius

Pisces

# Aries as a Fire Sign

Zodiac signs are also grouped according to the four **classical elements**. These are fire, earth, water, and air. Signs that belong to the same group share common personality traits.

Aries is a fire sign. Fire people are **spontaneous**. They live in the moment and are always looking for fun things to do. Fire people are considered to be passionate and energetic. They can also be moody.

Fire people are known for their ability to create fun moments for those around them, no matter what they are doing.

# Zodiac Signs
## by Element

# Being an Aries

An Aries' fire traits and cardinal qualities combine to create a specific type of person. A key Aries strength is enthusiasm. Aries are able to motivate the people around them on the basis of personality alone. People are drawn to their charm and **charisma**.

Aries have their weaknesses as well. They are known for being impatient. They love to be in the center of the action, but become frustrated when problems get in the way of moving forward. This can cause them to become short-tempered with others.

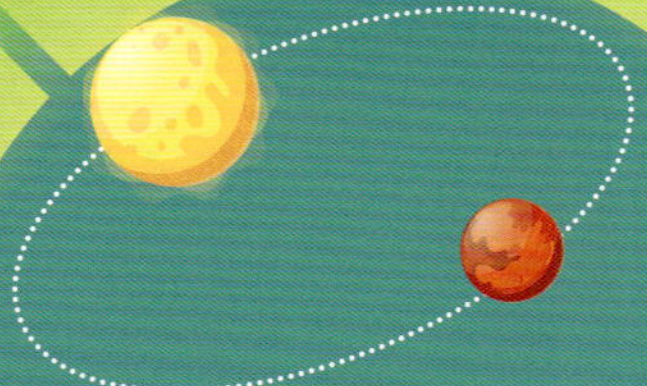

**Mars** is Aries' ruling planet. Mars is the **second-smallest planet** in the solar system.

The zodiac is divided into **12** houses. **Aries is the ruler** of the **first house**, the house of self.

People gravitate toward Aries because of their positivity and ability to build a sense of community.

# Aries through Time

Aries have had a significant impact on the world over time. They have made important discoveries, written beloved stories, and set athletic records. Their contributions have helped make the world what it is today.

**193**

**Septimius Severus** (born April 11, 146 AD) is proclaimed emperor of the Roman Empire. During his reign, the empire expands to cover more than 2 million square miles (5.2 million square kilometers).

Dutch scientist **Christiaan Huygens** (born April 14, 1629) discovers that Saturn is a ringed planet after viewing its rings through a telescope he developed.

**1659**

**1800**

**Thomas Jefferson** (born April 2, 1743) is elected to become the third president of the United States.

**1835**

*Tales, Told for Children* by **Hans Christian Andersen** (born April 2, 1805) is published. It includes such classic fairy tales as "The Tinderbox" and "The Princess and the Pea."

**1954**

Athlete **Roger Bannister** (born March 23, 1929) becomes the first person to run 1 mile (1.6 km) in under four minutes.

**2020**

*Once Upon a Time in Hollywood*, directed by **Quentin Tarantino** (born March 27, 1963), wins the Golden Globe Award for Best Motion Picture, Musical or Comedy.

# Making Friends

Some people think that zodiac signs can predict how people will relate to one another. Each sign has different traits. Certain signs may be more **compatible** than others. An Aries may be able to tell if a person will be a good friend just by knowing his or her sign.

## It's Friendship

**Aries get along well with people born under these signs.**

Aries

Aquarius

Libra

# It's Love

Aries often find romance with these signs.

Gemini

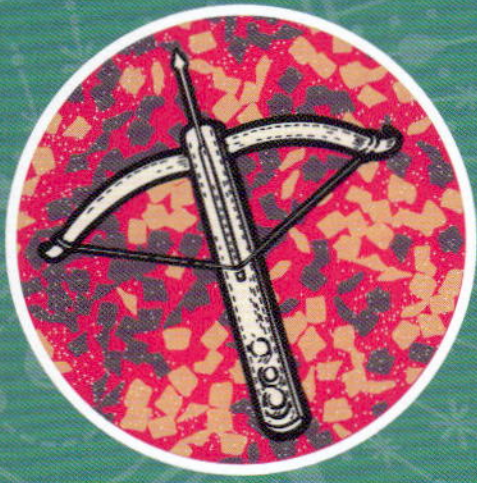

Sagittarius

Leo

# It's Complicated

Aries find it difficult to form bonds with these signs.

Virgo

Cancer

Capricorn

# Know Your Aries

Aries continue to make an impact on the world. They can be found doing good work in various fields. Did you know these people are Aries?

## Lady Gaga

**Born:** March 28, 1986

Born Stefani Joanne Angelina Germanotta, this singer, songwriter, dancer, and actor first began performing as a teenager in New York. She has since gone on to sold-out concerts, numerous music awards, and three **Oscar** nominations. Her Born This Way Foundation aims to inspire youth and build better communities.

In 2019, Lady Gaga won an Oscar for the song "Shallow." It was featured in the movie *A Star is Born.*

## Kyle Lowry

**Born:** March 25, 1986

Kyle Lowry showed an early talent for basketball. He played point guard in high school and was ranked sixth in the national standings. In 2006, he was drafted by the Minnesota Grizzlies. By 2012, he was with the Toronto Raptors, where he played a key role in the team's 2019 National Basketball Association (NBA) championship win.

## Saoirse Ronan

**Born:** April 12, 1994

Raised in Ireland, Saoirse Ronan began acting at an early age, appearing in Irish television shows. Her career launched in earnest with the 2007 film *Atonement*, for which she received her first of four Oscar nominations. Her lead roles in movies such as *Lady Bird* and *Little Women* have won her fans worldwide.

## Chance the Rapper

**Born:** April 16, 1993

Chancelor Bennett started rapping in sixth grade. By the age of 19, he was considered one of Chicago's best rappers. Known for his independent nature, Chance the Rapper has mapped his own course in the music industry. This approach has brought him three **Grammy Awards** and several other accolades.

## Jane Goodall

**Born:** April 3 ,1934

Jane Goodall went into the jungles of Tanzania to study chimpanzees at the age of 26. By 1965, she had earned her doctorate in **ethology**. Goodall was one of the first scientists to immerse herself in the lives of her subjects. She gave them names and recognized their unique personalities. In 1977, she co-founded the Jane Goodall Institute, which preserves **habitats** for chimpanzees in Africa.

# The Aries QUIZ

**1** Between which two dates is an Aries said to be born?

**2** How many stars make up the main shape of the Aries constellation?

**3** With which Greek myth is Aries most linked?

**4** What are the three qualities of the zodiac?

**5** To which element group does Aries belong?

**6** Which house of the zodiac does Aries rule?

**7** Which Aries became the first person to run a mile in less than four minutes?

**8** Which animals did Jane Goodall study in Tanzania?

ANSWERS: 1. March 21 and April 19 2. 4 3. Myth of the golden fleece 4. Cardinal, fixed, and mutable 5. Fire 6. The first house, the house of self 7. Roger Bannister 8. Chimpanzees

# Key Words

**charisma:** the ability to attract the attention and admiration of others

**classical elements:** materials from which all other materials were once believed to be made

**compatible**: capable of existing together in harmony

**constellations:** groups of stars that form patterns in the sky

**ethology:** the science of animal behavior

**fleece:** the woolly covering of a sheep or goat

**Grammy Awards:** annual awards given to recognize achievements in the music industry

**habitats**: the natural homes of organisms

**myth:** a story that was made up in the past to explain natural events

**orbit:** a regular, repeating path that one object in space takes around another

**Oscar**: an award given to recognize achievements in the film industry

**qualities:** traits that make a person or thing what it is

**spontaneous:** happening in a sudden way without any planning

# Index

# Get the best of both worlds.

AV2 bridges the gap between print and digital.

The expandable resources toolbar enables quick access to content including **videos**, **audio**, **activities**, **weblinks**, **slideshows**, **quizzes**, and **key words**.

**Animated videos** make static images come alive.

Resource icons on each page help readers to further **explore key concepts**.

Published by AV2
14 Penn Plaza 9th Floor
New York, NY 10122
Website: www.av2books.com



Library of Congress Control Number: 2020938549

ISBN 978-1-7911-2616-2 (hardcover)
ISBN 978-1-7911-2617-9 (softcover)
ISBN 978-1-7911-2618-6 (multi-user eBook)
ISBN 978-1-7911-2619-3 (single-user eBook)

Printed in Guangzhou, China
1 2 3 4 5 6 7 8 9 0 24 23 22 21 20

062020
101119

Editor: Heather Kissock
Designer: Terry Paulhus

Every reasonable effort has been made to trace ownership and to obtain permission to reprint copyright material. The publisher would be pleased to have any errors or omissions brought to their attention so that they may be corrected in subsequent printings.

The publisher acknowledges Getty Images, iStock, Shutterstock, and Wikimedia as its primary image suppliers for this title.